THE VIETNAM WAR

Frontline Soldiers and Their Families

Sarah Levete

Gareth Stevens PUBLISHING

Please visit our website, **www.garethstevens.com**. For a free color catalog of all our high-quality books, call toll free 1-800-542-2595 or fax 1-877-542-2596.

Library of Congress Cataloging-in-Publication Data
Levete, Sarah.
The Vietnam War: frontline soldiers and their families / by Sarah Levete.
p. cm. — (Frontline families)
Includes index.
ISBN 978-1-4824-3061-5 (pbk.)
ISBN 978-1-4824-3064-6 (6 pack)
ISBN 978-1-4824-3062-2 (library binding)
1. Vietnam War, 1961-1975 — Juvenile literature. I. Levete, Sarah. II. Title.
DS557.7 L48 2016
959.704—d23

First Edition

Published in 2016 by
Gareth Stevens Publishing
111 East 14th Street, Suite 349
New York, NY 10003

© 2016 Gareth Stevens Publishing

Produced by Calcium
Editors for Calcium: Sarah Eason and Rachel Warren Chadd
Designers: Paul Myerscough and Jessica Moon
Picture researcher: Susannah Jayes

Picture credits: Cover: National Archives and Records Administration; Inside: Dreamstime: Jorisvo 7, Angela Ostafichuk 42; Shutterstock: Lefteris Papaulakis 6, Migel 39, Bill Ragan 41t, Sippakorn 38, Xuanhuongho 34, 44l; Wikimedia Commons: 8, 16, Library of Congress 24c, 33, Lycurgus 11, National Archives and Records Administration 1, 4, 5, 10, 14, 15, 17, 22, 27, 29, 30, 32, 35, 37tl, 37tr, Texas Tech University 21, U.S. Department of Defense, 36, 44r, U.S. Information Agency 12, 13, 18, U.S. Marine Corps 23, U.S. Navy 41b, U.S. Navy National Museum of Naval Aviation 19, Uwdigitalcollections 28.

Printed in the United States of America
CPSIA compliance information: Batch #CS15GS: For further information contact Gareth Stevens, New York, New York at 1-800-542-2595.

CONTENTS

CHAPTER 1

THE VIETNAM WAR

The Vietnam War lasted just over 20 years. The fighting and bombing killed and injured millions of people from several different countries, and the horrific experience of the long war caused millions more to suffer from long-term mental disorders. For every one of those millions, there was a family who grieved for the death of a loved one or who had to come to terms with the effect of the war on their lives.

A Divided Country

The war pitted the United States against the communist North Vietnamese in a fight over South Vietnam. The Americans named the conflict the "Vietnam War." The North Vietnamese and their supporters named it the "American War," or, in full,

The Vietnam War brought death and destruction to homes across Vietnam.

the "War Against the Americans to Save the Nation." The North Vietnamese wanted to free South Vietnam from the influence of western countries and to bring it under communist control. The South Vietnamese government wanted to remain independent and allied to the United States and other western countries. The United States did not want South Vietnam to be taken over by communists. Civilians in South Vietnam were divided over what they wanted for their country.

Where Is Vietnam?

Vietnam is a narrow, S-shaped country in Southeast Asia. It borders China to the north, and the South China Sea runs along its eastern side, down to the Gulf of Thailand. Laos and Cambodia border the western side. Inland, large areas of Vietnam are covered in thick, dense jungle. This landscape was of huge significance for the fighting forces in the Vietnam War.

Families and the War

A baby born at the beginning of the Vietnam War would have reached his or her twenties by the end of it. For some children in Vietnam, the background to family life was constant fighting and hardship. Explosions, gunfire, and fear dominated their world. For people in the United States and other countries that sent troops to Vietnam, the war meant missing a parent, child, or other loved one, and living with the often terrible consequences of a ruthless conflict.

A young soldier guards a supporter of the North Vietnamese. The Vietnam War would change forever the lives of both men's families.

WHAT CAUSED THE WAR?

France, a colonial power, had ruled Vietnam since the nineteenth century. The start of World War II presented a Vietnamese communist named Ho Chi Minh—meaning "He Who Enlightens"—with the chance to prepare his country for independence from France. In 1941, Ho Chi Minh established the Vietminh (League for the Independence of Vietnam).

Vietnam Under Foreign Masters

In 1941, the Japanese took control of the countries under France's colonial rule, including Vietnam. The Vietminh fought against the Japanese and managed to take control of parts of North Vietnam. After the Japanese surrendered in 1945, Ho Chi Minh declared the country the Democratic Republic of Vietnam. However, the French returned in 1946, and there then followed a period of war in which the French army lost thousands of men in battle. France finally withdrew in 1954.

Lyndon B. Johnson
United States
8 cents

This stamp shows an image of US President Lyndon Johnson. Three other US presidents were in office during the Vietnam War, Eisenhower, Kennedy, and Nixon.

Trying to Solve the Problem

World powers, including the United States and the Soviet Union, came together in 1954 at an international gathering, called the Geneva Conference, to try to solve the conflict. It was agreed that communist Ho Chi Minh would control the North and an anticommunist named Ngo Dinh Diem would control the South. There would be elections, and Vietnamese people could decide in which part of the country they wished to live. However, Ngo Dinh Diem refused to hold elections.

The United States dreaded the spread of communism that had already divided another Asian country, Korea, into South and North. The US sent "advisors" to South Vietnam in an effort to stop this from happening again.

The Vietcong and War

In the North, the Vietminh had established strong control with the support of the peasant community. It had achieved this partly by giving back land to the peasants from wealthier landowners. Meanwhile, in the South, Diem's rule was corrupt and unpopular, and he was imprisoning his opponents. The Vietminh began to support those groups resisting Diem in the South. These groups went on to form the National Front for the Liberation of the South (NLF), more commonly called the Vietcong by the Americans.

Tensions and fighting increased between the North and South Vietnamese, with the United States sending more aid and military support to the South. In 1965, the US acknowledged it was at war.

This timeline shows a summary of key events in the long conflict. There is no agreed fixed date for the start of the Vietnam War because the involvement of the United States began long before it intensified its actions in 1965.

This newspaper headline confirmed the US government's decision to commit troops to the Vietnam War.

1954
July 21: Geneva Accords signed for the withdrawal of French and Vietminh to either side of boundary lines in Vietnam.

1955
February: President Eisenhower sends civilian and military advisors to train and support the South Vietnamese army.

1960
December 20: Formation of the NLF, known to Americans as the Vietcong.

1961
May: President John F. Kennedy sends 400 Special Forces troops to train and advise Ngo Dinh Diem's army in South Vietnam.

1962
Summer: Australia sends advisors, and later troops, to support South Vietnam. New Zealand does the same the following April.

1963
June 11: Buddhist monk Quang Duc sets fire to himself in protest at Ngo Dinh Diem's government's treatment of Buddhists (South Vietnam's religious majority). Diem attacks Buddhist pagodas.

November 1: Diem deposed and murdered in South Vietnam.

November 22: President Kennedy assassinated. Lyndon Johnson becomes president.

1964

January 30: General Nguyen Khanh seizes power in South Vietnam from General Minh.

August: In the Gulf of Tonkin, North Vietnamese boats attack US Navy destroyers. The US government approves the Gulf of Tonkin Resolution to wage war against North Vietnam.

1965

March 2: Operation Rolling Thunder, a three-year US bombing campaign against North Vietnam, begins.

1968

January 31: Tet Offensive–the North Vietnamese Army captures key cities and towns in South Vietnam.

March 16: Massacre of around 400 civilians at South Vietnamese village of My Lai.

May 10: Peace talks between the United States and North Vietnam begin–the start of a five-year process.

1969

January 20: Richard Nixon becomes President of the United States.

September 2: Ho Chi Minh dies.

1971

December: Last Australian combat troops leave Vietnam.

1973

January 15: Nixon announces cease-fire, which is followed by a peace agreement.

March 29: Last US troops leave Vietnam.

1974

August 9: President Nixon resigns and is replaced by Gerald Ford.

1975

April 30: North Vietnamese capture Saigon, capital of South Vietnam.

1976

July 2: Vietnam becomes one county–Socialist Republic of Vietnam. Saigon is renamed Ho Chi Minh City.

CHAPTER 2

A WAR OF MANY SIDES

The Vietnam War killed and injured millions of soldiers and civilians. Men and women on both sides of the conflict were directly caught up in the atrocities. Across the world, families felt the devastating impact of the war.

Generations at War

American soldiers had not long returned from fighting in the Korean War, which ended in 1953. In one generation, a father who fought in Korea might have then fought in Vietnam, and his son might also be called up to fight in Vietnam.

Primary Source: What Does It Tell Us?

This photograph shows Vietnamese peasants. They were caught between the communist Vietcong trying to take control of their country and the South Vietnamese and US troops trying to keep it under western influence. Family life was broken for many, as old and young found themselves living in a war zone. What effect do you think such a long war had upon the daily lives of families in Vietnam?

The Vietnamese had been involved in fighting France and Japan before the Vietnam War. All countries involved in the Vietnam War had already experienced the agonizing heartache and loss caused by a long conflict.

Fighting Lottery

To begin with, Americans did not have to join the army but could volunteer for service. However, as the involvement of the United States increased, men over the age of 18 were called up and had to serve in the army. This was known as the draft. Until 1969, people who went to college avoided the draft, but generally this was only affordable for families who were wealthy enough to pay for their child's education. This meant that many young men from poorer families, including many African Americans, were sent to Vietnam. In 1969, as the US government sent more troops to Vietnam, it introduced a lottery, drawn with blue balls, numbered with years. Men who were born in a particular year were called up to fight.

The United States army was supported mainly by troops from South Korea, Australia, New Zealand, Thailand, and the Philippines.

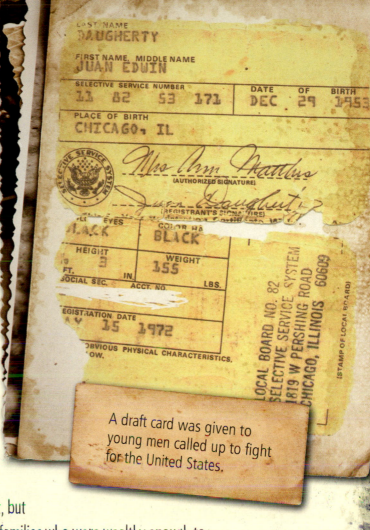

A draft card was given to young men called up to fight for the United States.

ON THE GROUND

The battlefield for the Vietnam War stretched right across Vietnam. Hundreds of thousands of troops from various countries scoured the land, engaging the enemy. Untrained fighters formed a key part of the North Vietnamese force—groups of communist sympathizers mainly from South Vietnam, known as the Vietcong.

Gaining Support

When Ngo Dinh Diem refused to honor the agreement of 1954 to hold elections, many South Vietnamese turned against him. As Diem persecuted those who disagreed with him, many of his opponents fled to the jungle, where Ho Chi Minh helped to organize them into the National Front for the NLF and supplied them with weapons.

North and South Vietnam

South Vietnam's army, the Army of the Republic of Vietnam (ARVN), was made up of poorly trained young men, who were forced to serve in the army for two years.

This girl and baby stand in the ruins of a building shattered by a bomb.

Primary Source: What Does It Tell Us?

This photograph shows the rescue of Vietnamese refugees after a Vietcong attack. Following the Geneva Conference's agreement to split Vietnam into two, an estimated 800,000 civilians fled North Vietnam to avoid living under communist rule. How do you think children coped with leaving their homes to start again, only to be thrown into a world of terror?

This was hard for their families, who relied on them to work the land. Many ARVN soldiers took their families to live with them in their camps. This meant they stayed together as families, but the conditions were poor.

The North Vietnamese army, however, was an efficient army. Young men were drafted in to fight and to help organize the support systems that enabled the army to travel with equipment and weapons to the south. They traveled on a network of mountain and jungle paths, called the Ho Chi Minh Trail.

Exploiting Children

Vietnamese children were often used to distribute propaganda leaflets, forced to help shelter soldiers from the enemy, and made to deliver messages and food. This posed risks to their safety from either of the opposing sides.

WOMEN AT WAR

Women fought for both the Vietcong and North Vietnamese Army (NVA). In the United States forces, women did not go into combat but worked in crucial areas, such as nursing and communication, and for aid organizations, including the International Red Cross. Women often endured the same harsh conditions as the soldiers. Many female journalists traveled to Vietnam to report on a war that divided American opinion.

Nurses in Vietnam

Ninety percent of the women in the US Army in Vietnam worked as nurses. The use of helicopters in the war enabled a quick transfer for injured soldiers to makeshift hospitals, where nurses had much greater responsibility for decision-making and treatment than in previous conflicts. These women saw and treated terrible injuries.

Primary Source: What Does It Tell Us?

This Vietnamese mother is protecting her child. Imagine the terror that the mother and her child must have felt during this war. They risked being targeted by the Vietcong for supporting the United States and its allies, they risked being killed in cross fire, and they risked being attacked by US soldiers if they were thought to be communist sympathizers. What do you think these helpless victims of the war felt about the conflict?

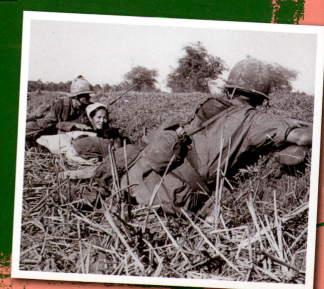

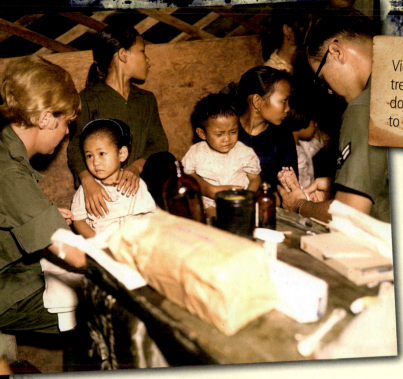

Vietnamese children receive treatment from a team of army doctors and nurses who traveled to villages to offer medical support.

Women had key roles beyond the combat zone. They were active in the community, providing health care for Vietnamese families. This became even more important as the war continued and families suffered from a lack of food.

Bringing Up Families Alone

When the men were fighting in Vietnam, mothers at home were left to bring up and care for their children. For American soldiers, a tour of duty was nearly one year long. The women left behind had to cope with the absence of their partner and suffer anxiety about their safety.

In North Vietnam, men were drafted to fight for the NVA. This meant that women had all of the responsibility and work of farming their land, as well as bringing up their children. Women were also expected to help protect villages in the North from American bombardment.

Changing Roles at Home

The civil rights movement that spread through the United States during the 1960s brought to light the inequalities faced by women as well as the inequalities that nonwhites had to endure. As the Vietnam War was being fought, the role of women was increasingly changing. In December 1961, to secure better rights for women, President Kennedy established the President's Commission on the Status of Women.

CHAPTER 3

CONDITIONS OF WAR

United States troops found it difficult to cope with the dense, hot, and humid jungle conditions. Also, despite their relentless bombing campaigns and sophisticated weapons, they were unprepared for their enemy's methods. The tactics on both sides were devastating for all the families, whatever side they supported.

Guerrilla Tactics

The eventual success of the NVA and Vietcong was due largely to their guerrilla tactics. The Vietcong improvized many of their weapons from whatever they could find. They used US bombs that had not exploded and created lethal booby traps, such as deadly sharp spikes hidden in the ground. The Vietcong had the advantage of knowing the land and being used to the conditions. They ambushed enemy soldiers and stayed so close to them that US forces were unable to attack them from the air without risking the lives of their own men.

A girl weeps for a family member after a mine laid by the Vietcong exploded, killing or wounding 15 people.

The Vietcong disguised themselves as peasants, the very people US troops were trying to protect. The Americans, therefore, began to suspect everyone, often with horrific consequences for innocent civilians and their homes.

Supplying Weapons

The Soviet Union and China supplied the NVA with weapons and rockets, which were then transported to the Vietcong along the Ho Chi Minh Trail. This was a jungle route the NVA had built through the neighboring countries of Laos and Cambodia. The Americans were at first reluctant to attack the Ho Chi Minh Trail because it could draw Laos and Cambodia into the conflict, further stretching US troops.

Hidden Networks

The Vietcong built a complex underground network of tunnels through which they moved from place to place, hidden from view. These tunnels were home to hospitals, training grounds, and army headquarters. When a network of tunnels was discovered, the US, Australian, or New Zealand army sent down one soldier, known as a tunnel rat, to try to blow it up. This was extremely dangerous, as the Vietcong laid booby traps in the tunnels.

LIVING WITH DANGER

For Americans, the Vietnam War, like World War I and World War II, was fought on foreign soil. Families suffered loss and anxiety about their loved ones, but day-to-day life in the United States, Australia, New Zealand, or South Korea was not under threat. However, in Vietnam, daily life was terrifying for everyone.

Constant Threats

Innocent people could walk over a Vietcong mine or be caught up in a US bombing raid and be killed or disabled for life. Simple tasks such as getting water from a well became terrifying and dangerous. Civilians running from bombs or gunfire were often shot.

Forced to Move

Diem, the South Vietnamese president, had put in place a very unpopular policy of forcing peasants to move to fortified villages, away from communist influence. The US army also created special areas where villagers were forced to move. These moves succeeded only in creating more support for the communists.

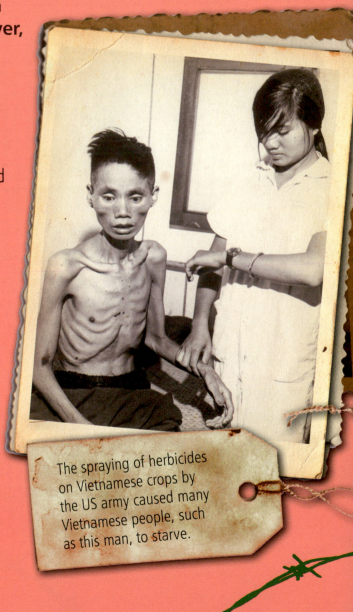

The spraying of herbicides on Vietnamese crops by the US army caused many Vietnamese people, such as this man, to starve.

Primary Source: What Does It Tell Us?

The drone of US bomber planes warned of impending danger, but, as the bombs fell, many civilians were killed. Between 1965 and 1973, US B-52 bombers dropped 8 million tons (7.25 million tonnes) of bombs on Vietnam. This is the same as dropping 300 tons (272 tonnes) for every man, woman, and child in Vietnam. What effect do you think this would have had on innocent civilians?

When US soldiers arrived in areas suspected of supporting the NLF or Vietcong, they often destroyed homes and villages. This encouraged more support for the Vietcong. Many families who had lived peacefully with other villagers now found themselves supporting the North Vietnamese, an alliance that put them in danger from the occupying troops.

Forced to Choose

Peasants in villages in South Vietnam faced terrible choices. If they supported the Vietcong or communists, and offered them shelter or food, they risked attack from the Americans. If they supported the Americans, they risked punishment from the NLF.

No Food

Vietnam depended mainly on farming for its economy. The US army sprayed a herbicide called "Agent Blue" onto crops in an effort to deprive the North Vietnamese of their food supply. Between 1962 and 1969, 688,000 acres (278,400 ha) of agricultural land were sprayed —mainly on fields of crops. During and after the war, food was scarce and families struggled to feed themselves. Twenty years of war shattered Vietnam's economy.

Troops from the United States, Australia, New Zealand, and South Korea were fighting a war miles from their homeland. United States troops were sent on tours of duty that lasted nearly a year. During that time, families at home witnessed some of the horrors of war on television and in newspapers. For every soldier or nurse fighting or working in Vietnam, there was a mother, father, sister, brother, wife, husband, or partner worrying about a loved one.

Contact with Home

Communication between the soldiers in Vietnam and families at home was mainly by letter, although some men were occasionally able to get to a telephone. Some letters were never sent, since the soldier was killed or captured before being able to mail it. Letters from one soldier,

Primary Source: What Does It Tell Us?

This letter was written in 1969 from serving soldier Carl Brauer to a friend. How do you think Carl Brauer's family felt when they had talked to him on the telephone?

August 11, 1969

Hi ..., I learned a lot of things since I came over here, one is HOME is a beautiful place and most of all the parents. I called home a couple of times and I talked to my mom and father and their voices sounded nice. It made us all feel a lot better inside to hear their voices.

Sergeant Steve Flaherty, came to light more than 40 years after they were written. A Vietcong soldier had taken them from the young man's body. "I felt bullets going past me," he wrote. "I have never been so scared in my life." In another letter, he wrote, "The NVA soldiers fought until they died and one even booby trapped himself, and when we approached him, he blew himself up and took two of our men with him."

Missing in Action

Families dreaded a knock at the door informing them that a family member had been killed. Some families still do not know what happened to their loved ones. These soldiers were described as "missing in action" (MIA). There are 1,642 US soldiers that remain unaccounted for. The fate of many Vietnamese soldiers is also still unknown.

CHAPTER 4

A BRUTAL WAR

The Vietnam War shocked the world with the brutality committed by soldiers on both sides and the extent to which innocent civilians were caught up in the fight. Those who survived the war were often wounded, physically or emotionally. The horror of the war would change their lives, as well as those of their families.

Shocking Sights

Young men were sent to Vietnam unprepared for what was to come. They saw fellow soldiers and friends suffer excruciating injury and death. They faced an enemy who evaded them with skill and savagery. They were part of a war that many people did not want to fight. Many soldiers carried out terrible and cruel acts. Soldiers returned home, often confused and damaged by their experience–and even addicted to drugs that had been readily available while on tour of duty.

A Vietnamese woman weeps over the body of her dead husband. She has lost the man she loves and the father of her children. Her life will never be the same again.

Primary Source: What Does It Tell Us?

Many men were taken as prisoners of war by the Vietcong and NVA, and they were often tortured and badly treated while in captivity. This photograph shows some men on their release. Not all the men were so lucky to survive. How do you think their families coped, knowing that a relative was held in terrible conditions by the enemy?

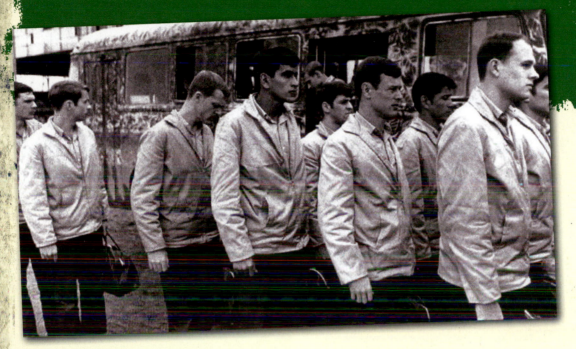

Help for Families

In 1965, Commander John Stockdale was leading an air raid over a North Vietnamese oil refinery when his A-4E Skyhawk plane was shot down. Stockdale landed in a rice field, where he was taken prisoner by the North Vietnamese military. He remained a prisoner of war (POW) for more than seven years, enduring beatings and torture. Back home, his wife Sybil campaigned for families of POWs to be given more information and support from the government and army about their captured relatives.

MASSACRED

During the course of the Vietnam War there were some terrible atrocities that ripped apart the lives of families. Americans were deeply shocked to see images and hear reports of their soldiers behaving in inhumane and callous ways.

My Lai Massacre

On March 16, 1968, US troops entered a South Vietnamese village called My Lai. They gathered together about 400 women, children, and elderly men, lined them up, and shot them. Perhaps the soldiers may have believed that the villagers had been helping the enemy, but there is no evidence of this. The soldiers killed innocent people. They took out their frustration, anger, and confusion at the lack of progress and success in the war on innocent civilians. They were angry that their Vietnamese enemy was often hidden but still deadly.

Images like this of the devastating grief families felt during the My Lai massacre sent shock waves around the world.

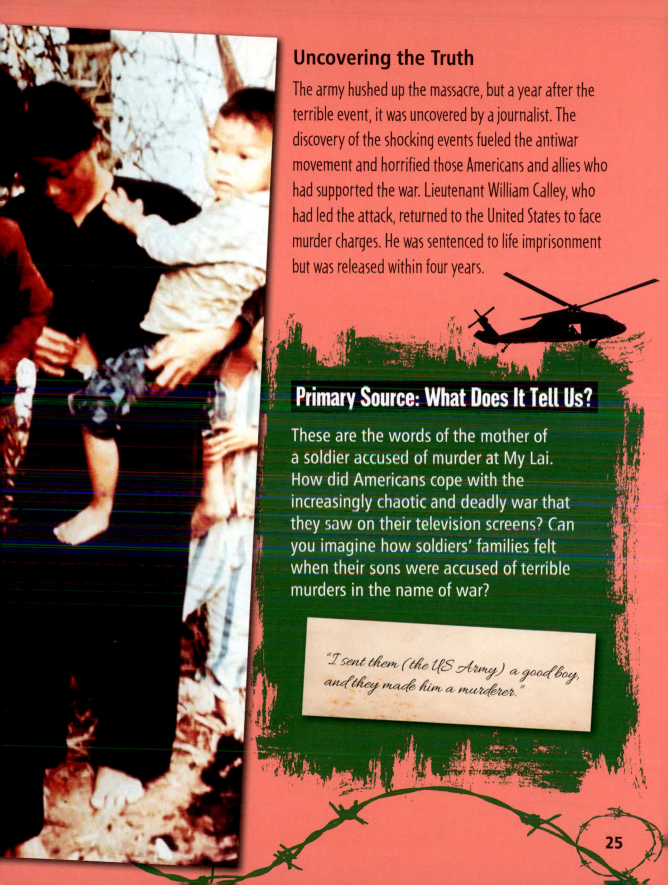

Uncovering the Truth

The army hushed up the massacre, but a year after the terrible event, it was uncovered by a journalist. The discovery of the shocking events fueled the antiwar movement and horrified those Americans and allies who had supported the war. Lieutenant William Calley, who had led the attack, returned to the United States to face murder charges. He was sentenced to life imprisonment but was released within four years.

Primary Source: What Does It Tell Us?

These are the words of the mother of a soldier accused of murder at My Lai. How did Americans cope with the increasingly chaotic and deadly war that they saw on their television screens? Can you imagine how soldiers' families felt when their sons were accused of terrible murders in the name of war?

"I sent them (the US Army) a good boy, and they made him a murderer."

YOUNG DEATHS

One of the most devastating and infamous images from the Vietnam War is of a terrified girl, naked, with her skin burned, running toward a photographer. This is the story of an innocent young girl whose life was turned upside down by the effects of the war in her country.

Kim Phuc—Victim of War

In 1972, nine-year-old Kim Phuc was living with her family in a South Vietnamese village, Trang Bang, over which the North and South Vietnamese were fighting for control. Kim was with her friends and family when a South Vietnamese airplane mistakenly started bombing a Buddhist pagoda in the village. The bombs were packed with napalm.

Napalm is a mixture of gasoline and a chemical, which creates a thick gel that sticks to the skin. When the gel is on fire, it burns for a long time, often burning victims through to the and bone, causing excruciating pain.

When the bombs fell, Kim, her friends, and her relatives ran. Two of Kim's young brothers were killed instantly. The napalm burned through Kim's skin. A Vietnamese photographer quickly snapped his camera to capture the image. He then whisked Kim to the hospital and remained in contact with her as she underwent numerous operations to heal the terrible burns that had eaten through to her bones. Kim Phuc was one of many thousands of children terribly wounded or killed in the war.

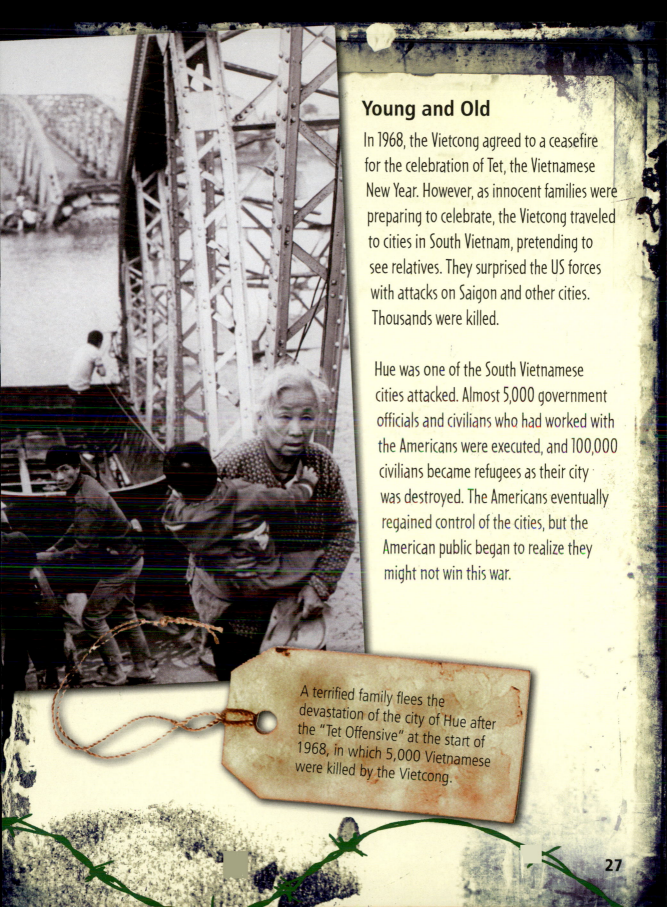

Young and Old

In 1968, the Vietcong agreed to a ceasefire for the celebration of Tet, the Vietnamese New Year. However, as innocent families were preparing to celebrate, the Vietcong traveled to cities in South Vietnam, pretending to see relatives. They surprised the US forces with attacks on Saigon and other cities. Thousands were killed.

Hue was one of the South Vietnamese cities attacked. Almost 5,000 government officials and civilians who had worked with the Americans were executed, and 100,000 civilians became refugees as their city was destroyed. The Americans eventually regained control of the cities, but the American public began to realize they might not win this war.

A terrified family flees the devastation of the city of Hue after the "Tet Offensive" at the start of 1968, in which 5,000 Vietnamese were killed by the Vietcong.

CHAPTER 5

LIVING WITH THE VIETNAM WAR

Until 1965, the United States' involvement in Vietnam was not clear-cut, although forces were active in the South. However, increased attacks on American troops pushed the United States into committing itself to a war to stop the spread of communism into South Vietnam.

A Divided Society

As the war continued with publicized disasters, such as the Tet Offensive, and little progress in stopping the North Vietnamese, many people both at home and in combat became increasingly disillusioned. The war exposed huge divisions in United States society. Some families were proud of their loved ones' bravery in fighting for their country; others were ashamed of the behavior of their soldiers.

Primary Source: What Does It Tell Us?

These protesters clearly show their angry feelings about the war. How do you think these protests made children feel, whose fathers were away fighting in the war?

People of all ages and backgrounds demonstrate, asking for the government to withdraw troops from Vietnam.

In Public View

The Vietnam War was played out in front of war reporters, photographers, and television cameras. Journalists and war photographers gave detailed descriptions of the horror of the war. The media spotlight threw a different light on the war. People around the world watched television images of young men dying and suffering catastrophic injuries. They saw shocking images of their soldiers treating other humans badly. Public opinion in the United States, Australia, and New Zealand was divided and led to angry demonstrations.

Growing Anger

On May 4, 1970, the US National Guard fired into a group of antiwar demonstrators at Kent State University in Ohio. Four students were killed. This sparked further antiwar demonstrations and riots on hundreds of other campuses.

A Protest Too Far

In New Zealand, some service families received terrible phone calls telling them that their loved one had been killed in the war. However, this turned out to be a cruel hoax by a group of antiwar protesters.

WAR HEROES?

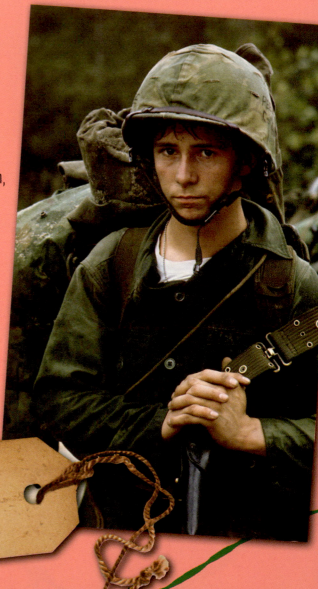

Often men returning home from war are called war heroes. This was not always the case for those men and women who had served in Vietnam. They often faced hostility, anger, and abuse. Some were spat at and even advised not to wear their uniforms in public.

Low Morale

Many of the United States soldiers were disillusioned about the war while they were in Vietnam. To cope with the horror of their experience, some turned to drugs that were easily available. These soldiers returned to the United States, often with a serious addiction to drugs. As the withdrawal of forces began, the mood among the troops dropped even more, as they knew they risked being killed in a war they were not going to win.

A Long Decline

Peace talks began in 1968 but they never amounted to more than talk. When Richard Nixon became US President in 1969, he committed to withdrawing American troops from Vietnam.

Young soldiers returned from a year's long service, often to find themselves blamed for the war.

To support this, he announced the policy called "Vietnamization"–training and equipping the South Vietnamese military to enable the United States to reduce troop numbers. Over the following three years, more than 500,000 soldiers were withdrawn.

Fighting at Home

People from poorer backgrounds, often within ethnic minorities, were less likely to be able to go to college and avoid the draft. This meant that a high proportion of young black men from the United States fought in the Vietnam War. Back home, their families were struggling to live in a country in which they did not have equal rights. Racial segregation (separating people according to ethnic background) ended only in 1964.

During the mid-1960s, there were serious riots in the United States, with people protesting at poor housing and lack of money for schools and hospitals. Many people linked these issues to the vast amounts of money soaked up to fund the war.

Vietnam war veterans often found it difficult to adjust to life back home, where many people did not consider them to be heroes.

DEEP WOUNDS

Many Vietnam War soldiers returned to their home country and resumed strong relationships with their families, found employment, and were as content as anyone else. However, others faced continued difficulties because of their experiences during the war. This in turn had a huge effect on their families.

Agony After the War

Many men suffered from post-traumatic stress disorder (PTSD) after the Vietnam War, with nightmares, flashbacks, and mental health issues. Their tour in Vietnam had been too traumatic —witnessing terrible deaths and wounding of comrades, seeing killing all around them, living with the fear of an unseen enemy. Often, the PTSD was so severe that the returning soldiers were unable to find work, hold down a job, or maintain close relationships.

Many Vietnam veterans could not cope with normal life and ended up sleeping on the street.

President Gerald Ford announces an amnesty for the thousands of men who had avoided the draft, many of whom had fled to neighboring Canada.

Families longed for the return of their loved ones. Their expectation was to resume family life as it had been before the war. However, men and women suffering from PTSD were often withdrawn, moody, and unpredictable. This had a damaging effect on their partners, parents, and children.

Issuing a Pardon

In 1974, US President Gerald Ford offered "draft dodgers" and deserters an amnesty —they would not be prosecuted for deliberately avoiding service in the armed forces. Ford stated that "reconciliation calls for an act of mercy to bind the nation's wounds and to heal the scars of divisiveness."

Primary Source: What Does It Tell Us?

Some men were given a "dishonorable discharge" when they left the army. This meant they left with a bad record, or "paper," perhaps for bad behavior. Many argued that this was due to undiagnosed PTSD. Today, many veterans campaign for their discharges to be made "honorable." These are the words of one US soldier discharged dishonorably. What effect do you think a dishonorable discharge had on men and their families?

"But after I came home from Vietnam, I couldn't even get my job back as a dishwasher because of my bad paper ... My discharge status has been a lifetime scar."

CHAPTER 6

LIVING WITH THE END

As the United States began to realize it could not win the war, it started to withdraw from South Vietnam. In 1973, the last troops left—the American men were coming home. However, in Vietnam the fighting was far from over. For Vietnamese families, the horror of the war continued long after the troops pulled out.

Weaknesses in South Vietnam

Within nine months, a ceasefire that had been agreed earlier was quickly broken. Without the strength of the US army behind it, the South Vietnamese army struggled. Its leaders were often corrupt and ineffective. The North Vietnamese advanced on the south with relentless force. In 1975, South Vietnam surrendered to North Vietnam. North Vietnamese troops entered Saigon, which was later renamed Ho Chi Minh City.

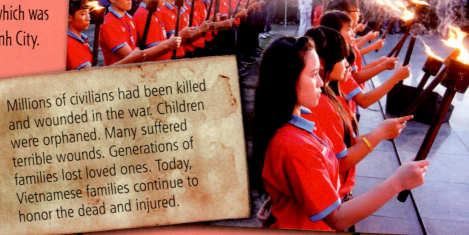

Millions of civilians had been killed and wounded in the war. Children were orphaned. Many suffered terrible wounds. Generations of families lost loved ones. Today, Vietnamese families continue to honor the dead and injured.

Primary Source: What Does It Tell Us?

In Vietnam, cities were bombed, and villages and fields were destroyed. How could this young man begin to resume normal life after the horrors he has experienced? What difficulties does a shattered community face when it tries to rebuild itself after a war?

Vietnam became a unified country under the control of North Vietnam's government, with Hanoi as its new capital. On July 2, 1976, North and South of the country became one nation, named the Socialist Republic of Vietnam (SRV).

A Long Road

American and other returning troops had to rebuild their lives back in their home countries, but the Vietnamese had to rebuild their country as well as their lives. Hundreds of thousands of South Vietnamese were killed. Millions more were sent to "reeducation camps," which were, in reality, prison camps. There, they had to suffer terrible conditions and physical abuse. Yet more families were torn apart, as their loved ones were killed or died in the reeducation camps.

Vietnamese men and women had been at war with each other. It would take a long time for the country to be free from the memory of the constant brutality.

FLEEING VIETNAM

As the North Vietnamese advanced on Saigon, the Americans desperately airlifted any remaining personnel from the city. There were chaotic scenes as many South Vietnamese tried to leave the country.

Escaping from Horror

Many people wanted to leave Vietnam. Some wanted to escape the poverty that the war had brought to the country. Others wanted to escape persecution from the winning communists. The refugees became known as "boat people," as they took to the seas to escape and begin new lives. Over two million Vietnamese sought to leave their country.

Fleeing on Boats

The desperate refugees often traveled in small, overcrowded fishing boats, hoping to settle in other countries. Many died before reaching dry land. Pirates attacked their boats, stealing and killing. Storms battered the flimsy fishing boats, and countless refugees drowned.

Primary Source: What Does It Tell Us?

This photograph shows Vietnamese refugees packed onto a small boat. Men, women, and children are passengers on this flimsy boat that had to withstand strong waves in the South China Sea. Assuming the refugees from the Vietnam War survived the journey to another country, what challenges do you think the families would have faced on arrival in another country?

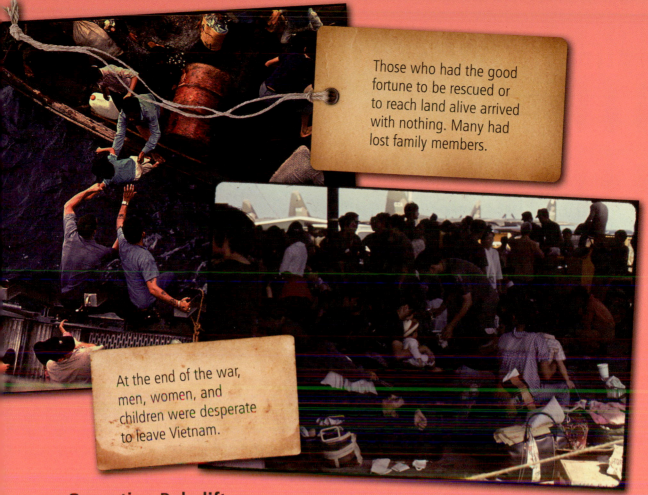

Those who had the good fortune to be rescued or to reach land alive arrived with nothing. Many had lost family members.

At the end of the war, men, women, and children were desperate to leave Vietnam.

Operation Babylift

In April 1975, Saigon was falling to the communists. There were rumors that people associated with the United States might be massacred. President Gerald Ford announced plans to evacuate 2,000 orphans. This was named Operation Babylift. Tragically, the first official flight crashed in the rice fields outside Saigon, killing around 140 people, most of them children. However, the evacuation continued for another three weeks.

Separated from Family

Grandparents, uncles, aunts, brothers, sisters, and parents might have been separated in the desperation to leave Vietnam. Once the war was over, families had to come to terms with the way their lives had changed forever.

BEYOND VIETNAM

The Vietnam War ended for American soldiers in 1973. For Vietnamese families, the chaos and fear of war continued for many more years. War also spread to the neighboring countries of Cambodia and Laos. President Nixon had begun to bomb Cambodia in 1969 because its jungle border had been used as a base for attacks on the South Vietnamese army and its allies and as a route to transport men and equipment into South Vietnam.

The United States Invades

In 1970, South Vietnamese and US troops invaded Cambodia, but without success. The North Vietnamese began to offer support to the Khmer Rouge, the Cambodian communist guerrilla force. The Khmer Rouge engaged in a brutal battle with the now pro-American regime in Cambodia. The effects were devastating.

Cambodian Crisis

The Khmer Rouge were eventually successful, and this started a terrible period for Cambodians, and indeed for the Vietnamese. The communist regime was brutal, murdering anyone considered unsympathetic to its views. Up to two million people are estimated to have died at the hands of the Khmer Rouge.

The Khmer Rouge killed ruthlessly and in vast numbers, as shown by this mass of skulls.

Hundreds of thousands of Cambodians fled the country with horrifying tales of violence. The Khmer Rouge led raids on Vietnamese villages along its borders, forcing Vietnamese families to flee their homes. Within five years, Vietnam itself had invaded Cambodia. This war with Cambodia led to the deaths of yet more young Vietnamese.

Secret Bombing

In 1964, fearing the spread of communism in Laos (a neutral country), the United States had begun a secret nine-year bombing campaign. It dropped 260 million bombs on the country, which were meant to explode when they hit the ground. However, many did not. They remained hidden in the ground, exploding unexpectedly. An average of 300 Lao people are injured or killed by these weapons every year.

An unexploded bomb hangs outside a restaurant, a grisly reminder of the "secret war" against Laos.

BOMBIE RESTAURANT & BAR

CHILDREN OF THE WAR

During the long war, many American troops or men working in civilian roles had met Vietnamese women. As a result of these relationships—some very short and others more serious—children were born. These half-Vietnamese, half-American children became known as "Children of the Dust" or "Amerasians."

Abandoned Children

When the NVA advanced on South Vietnam, and US troops and other personnel had left, the women and their Amerasian children were abandoned. These mothers were often shunned by their own communities for having had relationships outside marriage. They faced hostility for their relationships with the enemy. Some of the women panicked and rejected their babies or children.

Left in Vietnam

For those abandoned children, life was often a struggle. Their different appearance led to discrimination. In 1982, the US Congress passed the Amerasian Immigration Act, which allowed Vietnamese Amerasians to emigrate to the United States. Some children attempted to find their fathers, while others simply wanted to build new lives.

Fate of the Refugees

Waves of people fled Vietnam. Initially, it was those who wanted to escape the advancing NVA and communist rule. Later, when the new Vietnamese government passed a law that targeted people of Chinese descent, many Vietnamese with Chinese ancestry left the country.

Life as a refugee was hard. Children were haunted by the memories of the war and challenged by the hardship of starting a new life in another country.

Refugees who survived the journey to another country faced an uncertain future. Many had to live in overcrowded refugee camps before host countries decided whether or not to accept them. Governments were not always willing to accept people who came with nothing and needed support. Some were sent back to Vietnam to face an uncertain future. Those who were allowed to stay often faced hostility from people who lived in the host country. Some countries struggled to provide the home, education, and health care that all families need.

Primary Source: What Does It Tell Us?

These refugees are boarding a US military ship. What do you think their lives were like when they arrived in a foreign country and had to find new homes and work? How do you think having to make a new life in a new country after surviving the horrors of the war might have affected them further?

DEFORMITIES AND DEATH

It is more than 40 years since the Vietnam War. However, the war has affected the health of survivors since then and continues to do so today. Shortly after returning home, Vietnam veterans began to suspect that their sickness or the instances of their wives having miscarriages or children born with birth defects may have been related to "Agent Blue," "Agent Orange," and the other toxic herbicides they were exposed to in Vietnam. Veterans began to file claims for compensation, but they had to prove that the symptoms of sickness had begun within a year of leaving the army.

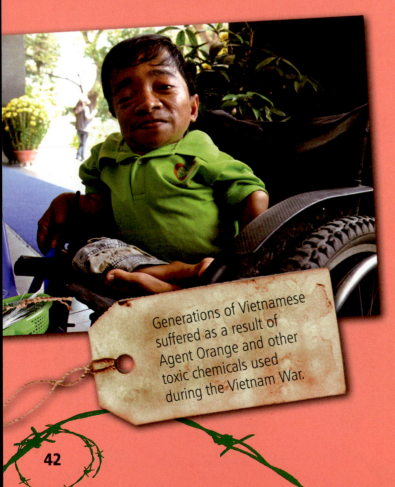

Generations of Vietnamese suffered as a result of Agent Orange and other toxic chemicals used during the Vietnam War.

Toxic Effect

Vietnam is covered in dense jungle —the perfect hiding place for the Vietcong. During the war, the United States decided to destroy this jungle cover. One of the chemicals used was known as "Agent Orange." In 1969 alone, 2,555,810 acres (1,034,300 ha) of forest were destroyed using Agent Orange. The effect of the chemical spread farther than the jungle. Many Vietnamese children were born with birth defects caused by their parents' exposure to Agent Orange.

Make It Count

Lynne Hawkins's husband, Laurie, served with the New Zealand army in Vietnam. She believes his death in 1996 was caused by the effect of Agent Orange and that such deaths should be added to the number of war casualties. Lynne traveled to the Vietnam Veterans Memorial Wall in Washington, D.C., to place a poem there for her husband.

Not landmine, grenade nor bullet
Could permanently close your eyes.
It was the silent stealth of "The Agent"
That attacked from out of the skies.

You left me behind when we parted
At least you saw your sons grown.
You died in my arms as I held you,
Now the Lord has taken you home.

Secondary Source: What Does It Tell Us?

Vietnamese families are coping with generations of children born with disabilities as a result of the war. What do the words of Frank Susa from UNICEF tell you about the long-lasting effect of the war on people's health?

"Vietnam is home to a disproportionately large number of disabled children—including many affected by exposure to chemicals left over from the spraying of Agent Orange."

THE LEGACY OF VIETNAM

The Vietnam War killed and injured millions. Countless families were left grieving, and millions of children were orphaned. Much of Vietnam's land was destroyed, either by bombs or toxic herbicides, such as Agent Orange. Soldiers from Australia, New Zealand, South Korea, and Thailand, as well as the United States, were scarred forever by the shocking and traumatic experience of the war.

Was It Worth It?

The United States did not succeed in repelling the communists from South Vietnam. As a result, Americans questioned the morality of the war and the role played by their country. The confidence and pride of Americans were shaken, because the long and costly war saw them withdraw without success. Whether or not the war succeeded for the nations that took part, only individual families could say if their involvement in it had been worth the physical and emotional pain it caused.

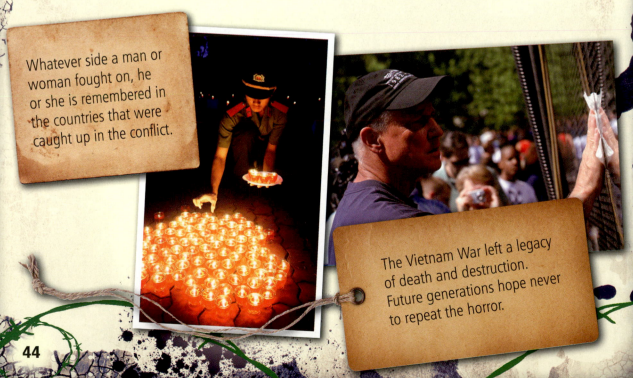

Whatever side a man or woman fought on, he or she is remembered in the countries that were caught up in the conflict.

The Vietnam War left a legacy of death and destruction. Future generations hope never to repeat the horror.

An American soldier, Jonas Freeman, served one tour of duty in Vietnam. What do his words tell you about how the reception soldiers received made their families feel?

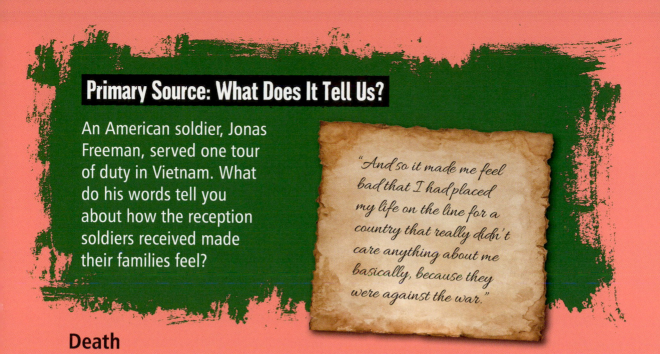

"And so it made me feel bad that I had placed my life on the line for a country that really didn't care anything about me basically, because they were against the war."

Death

These are the estimated death tolls for troops involved in the Vietnam War.

- South Korea: more than 4,000
- Thailand: 350
- Australia: more than 300
- New Zealand: 37
- North Vietnamese and Vietcong: 1.1 million
- South Vietnamese: 200,000–250,000
- United States: 58,200

Two million Vietnamese civilians were killed.

More than Politics

Beyond the politics, the Vietnam War was a long and appalling period for families throughout Vietnam, the United States, and its allied countries. The shocking death toll left millions of families mourning a loved one or coping with the traumatic emotional and physical problems faced by others.

GLOSSARY

amnesty official pardon

assassinate to deliberately kill someone

B52 US long-range heavy bomber airplane

booby trap deadly device hidden in a harmless-looking place

Buddhist someone who practices Buddhism, the main religion in South Vietnam

ceasefire command to stop attacks

civil rights movement movement in the United States organized mainly to give black Americans the same rights as white Americans

colonial rule when one country has control over another country

communist person who believes in creating an equal society through government control of property and many other areas of life

cross fire gunfire from two or more directions

deserters soldiers who abandon the army

draft system where people are called up to fight in a war

evacuate to help to leave

guerrilla tactics way of fighting using irregular tactics such as ambushes and booby traps

herbicide chemical used to destroy plants

Khmer Rouge ruthless communist guerrillas who fought in Cambodia and later ruled the country

morality rights and wrongs

napalm thick mixture of gasoline and chemicals used in bombs

neutral not allied to any particular side

post-traumatic stress disorder (PTSD) condition that can affect someone's mind after a terrible experience

propaganda information that tries to persuade people to believe one particular point of view

racial segregation separating according to race or ethnicity

reconciliation becoming friends again

refugees people who have to leave their home, and often their country, for their own safety

tour of duty length of time spent in a war zone

veterans men and women who have served in the armed forces

Vietcong men and women fighting in South Vietnam against the Americans and in favor of the North Vietnamese

Vietminh organization, also known as the League for the Independence of Vietnam, set up by Ho Chi Minh to free Vietnam from colonial rule

FOR MORE INFORMATION

Books

Benoit, Peter. *The Vietnam War* (Cornerstones of Freedom). New York, NY: Scholastic, 2013.

Caputo, Philip. *10,000 Days of Thunder: A History of the Vietnam War.* New York, NY: Atheneum Books for Young Readers, 2011.

Jeffrey, Gary. *The Vietnam War* (Graphic Modern History: Cold War Conflicts). New York, NY: Crabtree Publishing, 2013.

Websites

Learn more about the Vietnam War at:
http://encyclopedia.kids.net.au/page/vi/Vietnam_War

Discover more about the conflict at:
www.historynet.com/vietnam-war

Find out more facts about the war at:
www.factmonster.com/ipka/A0769991.html

Publisher's note to educators and parents: Our editors have carefully reviewed these websites to ensure that they are suitable for students. Many websites change frequently, however, and we cannot guarantee that a site's future contents will continue to meet our high standards of quality and educational value. Be advised that students should be closely supervised whenever they access the Internet.

INDEX